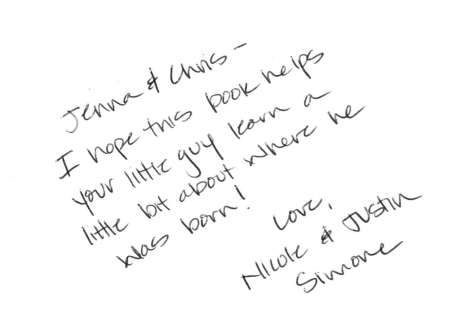

Jenna & Chris -
I hope this book helps
your little guy learn a
little bit about where he
was born!
Love,
Nicole & Justin
Simone

L is for Lone Star

A Texas Alphabet

Written by Carol Crane
Illustrated by Alan Stacy

Sleeping Bear Press™
310 North Main Street, Suite 300
Chelsea, MI 48118
www.sleepingbearpress.com

THOMSON

GALE™

© 2005 Thomson Gale, a part of the Thomson Corporation.

Thomson, Star Logo and Sleeping Bear Press are trademarks
and Gale is a registered trademark used herein under license.

Printed and bound in Canada.

10 9 8 7 6

Library of Congress Cataloging-in-Publication Data

Crane, Carol, 1933-
L is for Lone Star: a Texas alphabet / written by Carol Crane ; illustrated by
Alan Stacy.
p. cm
Includes bibliographical references. Summary: The letters of the alphabet are
represented by words, set in short rhymes with additional information, relating
to the state of Texas.
ISBN 1-58536-019-8
Texas—Juvenile literature. 2. English language—Alphabet—Juvenile literature.
[1. Texas. 2. Alphabet.] I. Stacy, Alan, ill. II. Title.

F386.3 .C7 2001
976.4—dc21   2001042895

For my editor, Heather,
and my three sons, great readers who have passed
on the love of books to our grandsons.

CAROL CRANE

To Mom and Dad in gratitude for showing me the world,
for teaching me what really matters in life, for the journeys
we have shared, and for believing in me. As my father
always said, "Anything is possible if you put your whole
mind and heart into it and believe in yourself!"

Thanks to Heather Hughes and Sleeping Bear Press for the opportunity
to explore new artistic territory and to share the gift of creativity.

Deo gratia

ALAN STACY

Aa

SAMUEL HOUSTON

STEPHEN F. AUSTIN

The Texas capitol building opened in 1888. The Senate and House of Representatives make the laws here. The building is made of pink granite from a quarry in Texas. The Goddess of Liberty sits atop the capitol dome. The life-size statues of Stephen F. Austin, known as the "Father of Texas," and Sam Houston are honored here.

Austin, the capital of Texas, is located in the hill country region of Texas.

A is for Austin,
a capitol so tall.
Here laws are made,
pledging justice for all.

B is for Bluebonnet—
    roadside blossoms saying "Hello!"
      Our state's official flower
        greeting friends we want to know.

The pioneers traveling by wagon were greeted by this beautiful blue wildflower. The petals look like a woman's sunbonnet. It blooms in the spring and can be found along major Texas highways. Indian paintbrush, buttercups, Mexican hats, and many other beautiful wildflowers are also found throughout Texas. Ennis, Texas was named the official Bluebonnet City.

Ennis is located in the prairies and lakes region of Texas.

b B

C C

Longhorn cattle are the official large mammal of Texas. Cattle drives on the Chisholm Trail from 1865-1880 began at Red River Station on the north border of Texas. Cowboys would bring cattle in from areas all over south Texas as far away as Brownsville. Cattle were then driven on the Chisholm Trail from Red River Station to Kansas, where the railroad would take the cattle east.

Chili is the official state dish of Texas.

The Chisholm Trail started in the south Texas plains region and as far south as Brownsville.

C is for Cowboys and Cattle,
riding over the Chisholm Trail.
Chuck wagons, chili con carne,
at night a lonesome guitar tale.

In 1885, a young pharmacist experimented with different fruit flavors and the soda Dr Pepper was born. This was the beginning of the soda pop industry in America. There is a Dr Pepper museum in Waco, Texas.

Waco is located in the prairie and lakes region.

How good Fritos would be with soda! Originating from corn dough, corn chips were pressed and baked. In 1932, a Texas businessman baked the chips at night and then sold them by day, calling them Fritos.

D is for Dr Pepper—
over 100 years of soda to savor.
Invented in a drugstore,
mixing 23 different fruit flavors.

E e

Native Americans and Spanish explorers looking for gold used the "Pass of the North," crossing the Rio Grande River from Mexico into what is now Texas. El Paso was also a major stop for the Overland mail coach in 1858.

El Paso starts with E,
the "Pass of the North."
The Rio Grande crossing
where explorers set forth.

F is for Friendship—
we extend our hand to you.
This is our state motto—
please accept our friendship too.

"Texas" comes from an Indian word, "tejas." This means friend. Texas is larger than many countries in Europe. It is the second largest state in the United States. It has many landforms: mountains, prairies, beaches, deserts, rivers, lakes, forests, and wetlands. Texas has two time zones, central and mountain. It has many cultures, occupations, universities, museums, and state and national parks. Texas is "big" and welcomes everyone to the state with a "big" heart.

G is for Gemstone—
how beautiful you are.
Blue topaz is the state gem—
the cut is called lone star.

Blue topaz was adopted as the state gemstone in 1969. This natural mineral is found in Mason, Texas. Topaz is the November birthstone. The lone star design comes from the five-pointed star on the Texas state flag.

Mason, Texas is located in the hill country region.

g G

General Sam Houston, a Texas hero, gave his name to this great city. He was the first president of the "Republic of Texas."

Houston has a 52-mile inland shipping channel where ships come and go to all parts of the world.

Houston is also the earth's Space Capital. NASA's Apollo lunar missions were the first "Giant Leap" to the moon. The space center is named the Lyndon B. Johnson Space Center in honor of the 36th president of the United States. There are four presidents who were either born or lived in Texas: Dwight D. Eisenhower, our 34th president, Lyndon B. Johnson, our 36th president, George Bush, our 41st president, and George W. Bush, our 43rd president.

Houston is located in the Gulf Coast region.

H is for Sam Houston,
a legend of our state.
Houston, the largest city,
both mighty and great!

SAM HOUSTON · 1793-1863

LYNDON B. JOHNSON
36TH U.S. PRESIDENT

Six different flags have flown over Texas, each during a specific time over 482 years. (See list below.) The lone star flag, the official state flag, was created during the years of the Republic of Texas. The colors of the flag are red for courage, white for purity and liberty, and blue for loyalty.

Spanish 1519-1685
French. 1685-1690
Spanish 1690-1821
Mexican. 1821-1836
Republic of Texas 1836-1845
United States. 1845-1861
Confederate States 1861-1865
United States 1865-present

i I

Independence starts with I,
a big and important word.
Texas has been victorious—
freedom has been assured.

REMEMBER THE ALAMO

TEXAS ONE AND INDIVISIBLE

The official pepper of Texas is the jalapeño. (The chiltepin is the official native pepper.) More jalapeños are grown and eaten in Texas than any other state in the nation. The mockingbird, the state bird, eats chiltepin peppers when they are in season.

J is for Joplin, another **J** word. Scott Joplin was born near Linden, Texas in 1868. Even before studying with music teachers at the age of 11, he had taught himself to play the banjo and piano. His unique style of music called ragtime was a combination of Creole, African rhythms, and folk tunes. He was known as the "King of Ragtime."

J j

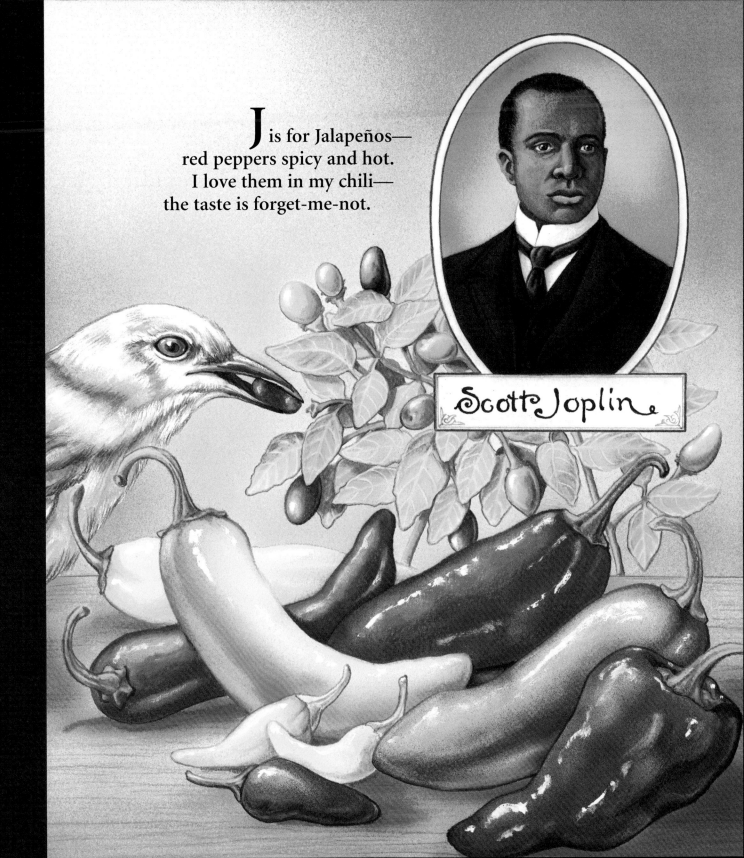

J is for Jalapeños—
red peppers spicy and hot.
I love them in my chili—
the taste is forget-me-not.

Scott Joplin

The kit fox and its pups live in a tunnel of dens. The underground dens stay cool in the hot summer. They like to roam the surrounding prairie grasslands. Other mammals that live in the panhandle region of Texas are the black-tailed prairie dog, the pronghorn, and the mountain lion.

k

K

K is for the Kit fox,
the smallest fox of all.
Lives in valley grasslands,
hunts only at nightfall.

L is for the Lightning whelk—
seashells on the Gulf shore.
Spiral shape, flashing streaks—
Oh look! I spy four more.

L l

The lightning whelk opens on the left side. It is named for its colored stripes. The lightning whelk is the official state shell of Texas.

Lightning whelks are found in the Gulf Coast region of Texas.

Also on the Gulf shores are many shore-birds. There are pelicans, egrets, whooping cranes, and roseate spoonbills.

Now, M is for Monarch butterfly
emerging with black and orange wings.
Flitting from flower to flower,
delicate beauty, life's cycle brings.

The monarch butterfly is the official insect of Texas. It is unique as it is the only butterfly to migrate in changing seasons like birds. It goes through four changes in form during its lifetime, from tiny egg, to caterpillar, to pupa, to beautiful butterfly. This takes about one month.

Do you see other **M** words?

The mockingbird is the state bird of Texas. It was adopted as the state bird in 1927. The songs of the mockingbird mimic other birds. Sometimes as many as 25 different songs are heard.

The Mexican free-tailed bat is the official state flying mammal. In Austin, a million bats take flight at dusk from under the Congress Avenue Bridge.

m
M

N is for the Nine-banded armadillo—
nature's brownish armored knight.
Our state's official small mammal—
his burrow a common sight.

Armadillos like to dig under the roots of bushes to find grubs to eat. They always give birth to identical quadruplets (four babies) and are the only animal to do that. River and stream banks are their favorite places to live. Armadillo means "little armored one" in Spanish.

N
n

Now, O is for the "Old three hundred"—
Stephen Austin led the way.
Pioneer families came for land grants—
good folks that he knew would stay.

Under the leadership of Stephen Austin, farmers traveled to Texas with the promise of land. These pioneers were from the southern states of Alabama, Arkansas, Louisiana, Missouri, and Tennessee. They settled along the Brazos, Colorado, and San Bernard Rivers where land was rich for growing crops and grazing cattle. They used the rivers for transportation.

P p

And **P** is for Pecan tree
with nuts so very good to eat.
The official tree of our state—
pecan treats are hard to beat.

The pecan tree is native to North America. Texas is the largest producer of native pecans. These trees can have a life span of 150 years, and can grow up to 150 feet tall! The soil conditions along Texas rivers are ideal for growing pecan trees. Pecans are nutritious and we all know that 10 million squirrels can't be wrong!

The prickly pear cactus is the official state plant of Texas. It is very pretty to see, but it is not fun to touch unless you are very careful. The fruit of the prickly pear is edible, and the branches or "pads" are also cooked and eaten as a vegetable. Have you ever tried prickly pear jelly or marmalade?

Quanah Parker was the last chief of the Comanches. He was a statesman, defending the rights of his people. He learned English and became a reservation judge. He was a friend to the people of his tribe and the white man as well.

Q is for Quanah Parker, Comanche Indian chief. Striving to lead his people, keeping his native belief.

q

Q

R is for the Rio Grande River
flowing wild, long, and free.
Its twisting turn named Big Bend—
an awesome sight to see.

EL CAPITAN (8078 FEET) IN GUADALUPE MOUNTAINS NATIONAL PARK

The Rio Grande River is the longest river in Texas. It begins in Colorado and flows to the Gulf of Mexico. For 1,200 miles it is the border between Texas and Mexico. The river's path winds through canyons and flatlands. The Rio Grande is at its widest in Big Bend National Park. When you step outside your car here, you will feel thirsty, as the air has the driest climate in Texas.

While there are many beautiful places to hike in Big Bend National Park, six of the tallest mountain peaks are located in Guadalupe Mountains National Park, near the New Mexico border. The tallest mountain peak in Texas is Guadalupe Peak, with an elevation of 8,749 feet.

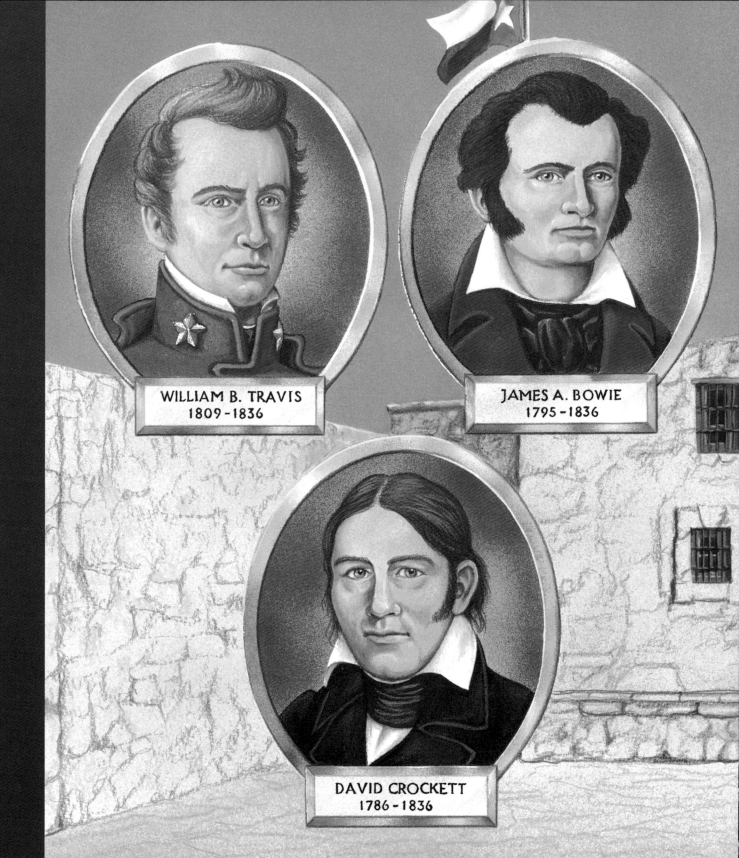

WILLIAM B. TRAVIS
1809-1836

JAMES A. BOWIE
1795-1836

DAVID CROCKETT
1786-1836

San Antonio is the second largest city in Texas. Davy Crockett, Jim Bowie, and William Barret Travis were all famous men that fought and died at the Alamo for freedom.

Today, the San Antonio River winds through the city for two and one-half miles. This part of the river through the city is called River Walk. In April, Fiesta Week is celebrated with music, food, dancing, a flower parade, and costumes. This is to commemorate the independence of Texas from Mexico.

San Antonio is in the south Texas plains region.

Now, **S** is for San Antonio,
home of the Alamo.
Today, with 35 bridges
the "Paseo del Rio".

Texas Rangers starts with T,
bringing peace to a countryside.
Riding throughout the state—
great men of courage and pride.

T t

The Texas Rangers are known for their skill and bravery. They are splendid horsemen, good trackers, and excellent marksmen. They were formed in 1823. There is a museum in Waco, Texas honoring these famous lawmen.

Many adventurous men came to Texas to strike it rich. Stories of those that made their dreams come true are written in the names of cities, towns, street signs, museums, libraries, and other notable places. Spindletop was the richest oil well and was located in the Gulf Coast region, near Beaumont. The piney woods region near Kilgore had the "World's Richest Acre" where 1,200 oil derricks stood. Some of those oil wells are still producing. This area was noted for its lumber and cotton.

Tyler, "The Rose Capital of the World," grows 500 varieties of roses. They are grown and shipped to all parts of the nation.

u
U

Underground starts with U,
secretly hiding black gold.
A derrick named Spindletop—
stories of oil wells are told.

V v

Valley agriculture starts with V—
northeast of the mighty Rio Grande.
Vegetables, fruit, and poinsettias too—
products of fertile Texas land.

Onions, lettuce, broccoli, carrots, tomatoes, and cabbage are all grown in the 330 days of perfect growing weather in the Rio Grande Valley. Aloe vera plants, poinsettias, and trees are sent to markets throughout the country.

The ruby red grapefruit is the state fruit of Texas. Rows of orange and grapefruit trees are found here.

The south Texas plains and the Gulf Coast region have perfect growing conditions along the Rio Grande River.

W is for windmills
spinning on a tower.
Some are pumping water,
others making power.

The early settlers of Texas needed water. Many of them had used windmills on their farms in the north and in European countries to pump water from nearby rivers. Windmills are found on many farms and ranches throughout Texas today. They are also for making electricity.

W
W

The XIT Ranch has a reunion rodeo every year. The capitol in Austin was built with money in exchange for XIT ranch land. This ranch is so large it took up land in 10 different counties. XIT means "Ten In Texas."

This event takes place in the panhandle plains region of Texas.

X X

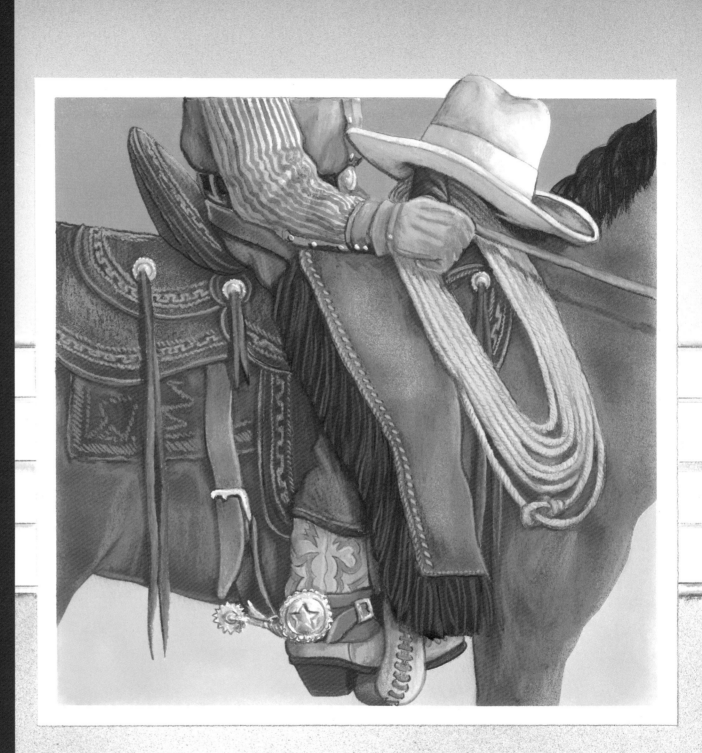

X is for XIT Rodeo—
saddles, hats, boots, spurs, and ropes.
One-handed bronc and bull riders—
cowboys with eight-second hopes.

Y is for Yucca—
tall soldiers with thorny swords.
Creamy with bell-shaped flowers—
A sweet scent is our reward.

Yy

Yucca plants come in many sizes, some short but others very tall, up to 20-40 feet. Many uses have been found for these plants. Baskets are woven from the leaf fibers, as well as rope, sandals, and mats. The buds and flowers are eaten raw or boiled.

Z is for the Texas Zoo—
javelina, eagles and deer.
All of our native animals—
can you find them here?

The Texas Zoo is located in Victoria, Texas. All of the birds, fish, mammals, turtles, and snakes living here are native to Texas. There are over 200 different species on display.

This zoo is found in the Gulf Coast region.

A Ten-Gallon Hat Full of Facts

1. Cotton was first grown in Texas by what group?

2. What is the official state reptile of Texas?

3. A musical instrument is one of the state symbols of Texas. What is it?

4. Langtry, Texas has a museum featuring what colorful Texas judge?

5. What is the nickname given General Sam Houston?

6. What is the official state stone of Texas?

7. What is the largest body of water completely within the boundaries of Texas?

8. What does Juneteenth celebrate?

9. What is the name of the area lying on either the eastern or western side of the Pecos River?

10. In 1680, Yselta Mission, the oldest mission, was settled near what city?

11. Why is Kemp's ridley sea turtle, a resident of the Gulf of Mexico, on the endangered list?

12. A 500 year old tree, the "Treaty Oak," stands in what city?

13. Texan Gail Borden Jr. invented the process for what kind of milk?

14. Where does Texas rank nationally in the production of watermelons?

15. Where does Texas rank in the production of wool?